MW01172667

1

<u>My New Life in Christ</u>

Now that I Have Trusted Him

George J. Quinn
Teaching Pastor, Friendship Bible Church
4004 Ocean Heights Avenue
Egg Harbor Twp., NJ 08234
www.friendshipbible.org

All scripture references are from the New American Standard Bible, **The Lockman Foundation**, La Habra, CA 1960, 1962, 1963, 1968, 1971, 1972, 1973, 1975, 1977 & 1995 unless otherwise noted.

My New Life in Christ
Now that I Have Trusted Him

Contents

Preface

This book is written for those who are prepared to come to Christ or have recently made a decision to trust Jesus for salvation. Making this decision is the most important choice you can make in life. When we trust in Christ, we begin a lifelong relationship with the best Friend we will ever know.

The first topic to be covered is the truth about becoming a Christian. The Bible tells us that...

> You are saved by grace through faith, and not of yourselves, it is the gift of God, not as a result of works, so that no one may boast. (Eph.2:8-9)

Believing that Christ died for our sins and trusting that for our forgiveness is how new life begins. The rest of this book is how to live after making that decision. Enjoy!

In His grip,
Pastor George
September 23, 2020

How to Use This Book

Although there is no "magic formula" for starting our new life in Christ, may I suggest some steps that could prove helpful in putting this book to good use?

1. Read each chapter carefully and answer the questions at the end. Check your answers with the key at the back of the book on page 69.

2. Read one chapter of the Gospel of John each day for the next 21 days.

3. Pray every day! Talk to your heavenly Father in Jesus' name and share whatever is on your heart.

4. There is a list of Bible verses to commit to memory on page 65. Copy these on note cards and carry them with you. Try to look at them often and remember them. This is called hiding God's Word in your heart.

Ready?
Begin!

My New Life in Christ
Chapter 1 - The Good News about Eternal Life

In order to have eternal life, we must **place our faith** in Jesus Christ. We are not able to earn salvation by our own efforts or by our good deeds. The penalty for our sin is death (separation from God). "For the wages of sin is death..." (Rom.6:23)

How can we be saved? Saved from what? Because of our sin, **we all deserve death**!

> For the wages of sin is death, but the free gift of God is eternal life in Christ Jesus our Lord. (Romans 6:23).

While the physical consequence of sin is physical death, that is **NOT** the only kind of death that results from sin. All of us have sinned against an eternal and infinite God.

> For all have sinned and fall short of the glory of God, (Romans 3:23)

We actually were born as **fallen creatures**. God's Word tells us we sin because of that fallen state. Because of that, the just penalty for our sin is also eternal and infinite. What we need to be saved from is **eternal destruction**.

> These will go away into eternal punishment, but the righteous into eternal life. (Matthew 25:46)

And if anyone's name was not found written in the book of life, he was thrown into the lake of fire. (Revelation 20:15)

However, **God demonstrated His love** for us by coming to the Earth in the Person of Jesus Christ to die in our place for all our sins.

> But God demonstrates His own love toward us, in that while we were yet sinners, Christ died for us. (Romans 5:8)

By placing our faith in **Christ alone** as the Lord who died and rose again, we receive the gift of "eternal life".

> These things I have written to you who believe in the name of the Son of God, so that you may know that you have eternal life. (I John 5:13)

All we have to do is ask.

> Whosoever will call upon the name of the Lord will be saved." (Rom.10:13)

Speaking about Jesus, Peter said, "...for there is no other name under Heaven that has been given among men, by which we must be saved." (Acts 4:12b)

Do we have to experience a new birth to know we are Christians? That is a **good question**. Jesus, speaking with Nicodemus, answers that question.

> Jesus answered and said to him, "Truly, truly, I say to you, unless one is born again he cannot see the kingdom of God." (John 3:3)

Without this new birth, **we are still lost** in our sin and with no hope of forgiveness. When we trust Christ, we ask God to forgive our sins and for Him to come into our lives and live His life through us. We become **new creatures** in Christ.

> Therefore if anyone is in Christ, he is a new creature; the old things passed away; behold, new things have come. (II Corinthians 5:17)

If you would like to **invite Jesus to be your Savior**, you could pray a prayer such as this, "Father, I want Jesus to be my Savior. I recognize that I am a sinner, but I believe that Jesus came and died on the Cross for my sins. Thank you for promising everlasting life to all who would call on Jesus' name."

If you have made that decision, **tell someone** who is a Christian so **they can rejoice with you** and keep you in prayer.

The Gospel of John records the Lord Jesus's words that contain **an amazing promise**:

> "For God so loved the world, that He gave His only begotten Son, that whoever believes in Him shall not perish, but have eternal life." (John 3:16)

Do we take God **at His Word**? Here we see a clear promise from God... "**whoever**" that is any one of us, "believes"... that is what is required, faith. **What** do we believe in? Jesus says, "...in Him"... that is believing in the Son, who He is and why He came. What are the results of trusting in the Son? The answer is he or she "will not perish, but have eternal life." That literally means, we will "never perish" but **shall have and hold eternal life**."

It cannot be any more clearly said! If we have trusted in Jesus Christ, we have eternal life with God. That life **starts now** and **goes on and on and continues into eternity**. When this life is over, that eternal life with God including the fact we will never perish goes on eternally. Praise God, our salvation is **secure**!

Well, now that you made that decision, **now what**? You've begun a new life in Christ. The "what" is really the content of the rest of this book! Our lives belong to Him and now we must live **responding to His leadership**. The joy and peace He gives will be a resource for us regardless of what we face from this point on.

My New Life in Christ
Chapter 1 - The Good News about Eternal Life
Thought Questions

1. How do we know that we are born again?

2. How can we know that we have eternal life?

My New Life in Christ
Chapter 2 - Know We Are His

When we trust in Christ, we begin a **lifelong** relationship with **the best Friend we will ever know**.

We are **living proof** that the **age of miracles** has not **passed**! For we, ourselves, are miracles. God's description of a Christian indicates that fact very clearly.

> Therefore if anyone is in Christ, he is a new creature; the old things passed away; behold, new things have come. (II Corinthians 5:17)

In chapter one, we reviewed the facts about the good news about eternal life. The task for this chapter is to **discover the value and strength** we find in our lives as we realize that we, those who have trusted in Christ, belong to Him now. The Bible says that we are now not our own, we are bought with a price. The Apostle Paul writes...

> For you have been bought with a price: therefore glorify God in your body. (I Corinthians 6:20)

As wonderful as that truth is, it is important that we **nourish** this new relationship with Jesus so that it has the **greatest possible impact** on our lives.

Our Lord Jesus made this truth His basic approach to one of the **most learned** men of His day – **Nicodemus**.

In the Gospel of John chapter three Jesus said to Nicodemus,

"You must be born again. If not, you'll never see the kingdom of God." (John 3:3)

Nicodemus raised an immediate objection. "**How can these things be?**" He was perplexed. This is the result of his unregenerated heart trying to analyze salvation.

> Nicodemus said to Him, "How can a man be born when he is old? He cannot enter a second time into his mother's womb and be born, can he?" Jesus answered, "Truly, truly, I say to you, unless one is born of water and the Spirit he cannot enter into the kingdom of God.
>
> That which is born of the flesh is flesh, and that which is born of the Spirit is spirit. Do not be amazed that I said to you, 'You must be born again.' The wind blows where it wishes and you hear the sound of it, but do not know where it comes from and where it is going; so is everyone who is born of the Spirit." (John 3:4-8)

Our Lord answered patiently, tenderly, "Nicodemus, you must be born again!" You can't explain it. You can't explain a lot of other things, either. **Take the wind**, for instance. Can you tell where it came from, or where it is going? No. You can feel it, hear it whispering through the leaves, but you can't explain it. Neither can you explain salvation.

Here's the difficulty, He continued, you were born once, with an earthly nature. You're a sinner, Nicodemus, and you have a sinful nature. That which is born of the flesh is flesh and nothing more! How do you ever expect to

16

get past the judgment of a holy God with nothing but sinful flesh?

You have to have another birth, Nicodemus, **a birth from above**. It is called a **birth of the Spirit**, because He's the One who is active in it. When that occurs, you'll have a **new, holy nature**, for that which is **born of the Spirit is spirit**.

Essentially salvation is a **miracle of receiving life**. There is nothing so hopelessly still as **a corpse**. No scientist has yet been able to breathe life into a dead body. Just as hopeless is the sinner without Christ. He is "dead in trespasses and sins." (Ephesians 2:1) There is not a prospect for doing any better, for "those in the flesh cannot please God." (Romans 8:8)

Our Lord Jesus emphasized this truth when He said:

> It is the Spirit who gives life; the flesh profits nothing; the words that I have spoken to you are spirit and are life. (John 6:63)

It is a sad fact that we have met hundreds of people who suppose **they can earn their way into Heaven** by becoming church members or by living a moral life, rather than having a personal relationship with Christ. These things are certainly commendable, but **they can't obtain eternal life** in Heaven with God.

The Bible tells us in Romans 6:23,

> "For the wages of sin is death, but the gift of God is eternal life in Christ Jesus our Lord." (Rom.6:23)

Heaven is a gift! In trusting the Gospel message, all we have to do is reach out and receive Jesus as our personal Savior and Lord, and Heaven is ours.

The reason for this is that **God's standard for Heaven is perfection**, yet **no one ever lived a perfect life**, **except Jesus Christ**. Sin separates us from God. The good deeds we may do can never overcome this gap or earn for us God's blessing.

Yes, a miracle happened to us when we were saved. The Lord Jesus touched our lives with His nail-scarred hand and gave us new life, with a new nature – **His life and His nature!**

Salvation is not something **we do**, but something **Christ does** when we receive Him. John writes,

> But as many as received Him, to them He gave the right to become children of God, even to those who believe in His name, (John 1:12)

Personal testimonies in the Gospels and the book of Acts highlight this fact.

Andrew talking to Simon Peter:

> He found first his own brother Simon and said to him, "We have found the Messiah", which translated means Christ. (John 1:41)

Philip to Nathanael:

> Philip found Nathanael and said to him, "We have found Him of whom Moses in the Law and also the

Prophets wrote—Jesus of Nazareth, the son of Joseph." (John 1:45)

The Samaritan woman at the well to her countrymen:

"Come, see a man who told me all the things that I have done; this is not the Christ, is it?" (John 4:29)

The Apostle Paul to King Agrippa:

While so engaged as I was journeying to Damascus with the authority and commission of the chief priests, at midday, O King, I saw on the way a light from heaven, brighter than the sun, shining all around me and those who were journeying with me. And when we had all fallen to the ground, I heard a voice saying to me in the Hebrew dialect, 'Saul, Saul, why are you persecuting Me? It is hard for you to kick against the goads.' And I said, 'Who are You, Lord?' And the Lord said, 'I am Jesus whom you are persecuting. But get up and stand on your feet; for this purpose I have appeared to you, to appoint you a minister and a witness not only to the things which you have seen, but also to the things in which I will appear to you; rescuing you from the Jewish people and from the Gentiles, to whom I am sending you, to open their eyes so that they may turn from darkness to light and from the dominion of Satan to God, that they may receive forgiveness of sins and an inheritance among those who have been sanctified by faith in Me.' "So, King Agrippa, I did not prove disobedient to the heavenly vision, but kept declaring both to those of Damascus first, and also at Jerusalem and then throughout all the region of Judea, and even to the Gentiles, that they should repent and turn to God, performing deeds appropriate to repentance. (Acts 26:12-20)

It is easy to see why this personal emphasis must be. **Only a Person** can reveal God to me:

No one has ascended into heaven, but He who descended from heaven: the Son of Man. (John 3:13)

No one has seen God at any time; the only begotten God who is in the bosom of the Father, He has explained Him. (John 1:18)

Only a Person could meet my personal need and heal sin's deadly sting:

As Moses lifted up the serpent in the wilderness, even so must the Son of Man be lifted up; so that whoever believes will in Him have eternal life. (John 3:14-15)

Only a Person – a divine Person could bestow eternal life:

For God so loved the world, that He gave His only begotten Son, that whoever believes in Him shall not perish, but have eternal life. (John 3:16)

And it takes **a Person** to satisfy and keep me:

And in Him you have been made complete, and He is the head over all rule and authority; (Colossians 2:10)

So then let no one boast in men. For all things belong to you, whether Paul or Apollos or Cephas or the world or life or death or things present or things to come; all things belong to you, and you belong to Christ; and Christ belongs to God. (I Corinthians 3:21-23)

When I approach God, I am **accepted** "in the Beloved":

To the praise of the glory of His grace, which He freely bestowed on us in the Beloved... (Ephesians 1:6)

And I realize that my righteousness now is **the righteousness He gives me**:

And may be found in Him, not having a righteousness of my own derived from the Law, but that which is through faith in Christ, the righteousness which comes from God on the basis of faith, (Philippians 3:9)

Salvation is not something – **it's Somebody**! When you were saved, you met a Person, you opened your life to Him, and you are now living under His control.

For this reason I also suffer these things, but I am not ashamed; for I know whom I have believed and I am convinced that He is able to guard what I have entrusted to Him until that day. (II Timothy 1:12)

You became part of **an eternal transaction**.

For what does the Scripture say? "Abraham believed God, and it was credited to him as righteousness." Now to the one who works, his wage is not credited as a favor, but as what is due. But to the one who does not work, but believes in Him who justifies the ungodly, his faith is credited as righteousness, (Romans 4:3-5)

Let us get the picture straight.

What does God demand? Righteousness

What can I offer? Only sin and more sin!

Can I ever hope to do better under my own power? No, I am condemned already without Christ.

> He who believes in Him is not judged; he who does not believe has been judged already, because he has not believed in the name of the only begotten Son of God. (John 3:18)

How may I obtain the righteousness that God demands? Simply by receiving it by faith!

> Even the righteousness of God through faith in Jesus Christ for all those who believe; for there is no distinction; (Romans 3:22)

When I receive Christ, does that **alter** my standing before God? **Certainly it does**! God takes the righteousness of Christ and puts it to my account. Because Jesus died for me He can be **just** and **the justifier** of all who believe.

For the demonstration, I say, of His righteousness at the present time, so that He would be just and the justifier of the one who has faith in Jesus. (Romans 3:26)

Namely, that God was in Christ reconciling the world to Himself, not counting their trespasses against them, and He has committed to us the word of reconciliation. Therefore, we are ambassadors for Christ, as though God were making an appeal through us; we beg you on behalf of Christ, be reconciled to God. He made Him who knew no sin to be sin on our behalf, so that we might become the righteousness of God in Him. (II Corinthians 5:19-21)

Who alone could settle the score of sin? God

Who was it, suffering on the cross for sin? God

Has the debt been paid? Yes, because:

And He Himself bore our sins in His body on the cross, so that we might die to sin and live to righteousness; for by His wounds you were healed. (I Peter 2:24)

Now why did we go into all these themes in a chapter entitled "Know We Are His"? The answer is we must develop **a confidence** in the fact that we belong to Him now and forever. As this confidence builds we develop a very important spiritual asset: **an assurance of our salvation**. When we place our faith in the Lord Jesus Christ for salvation and trust Him, we are forever held by

a grip that is stronger than any force in the universe. It is **God's grasp** on us forever!

> My sheep hear My voice, and I know them, and they follow Me; and I give eternal life to them, and they will never perish; and **no one will snatch them out of My hand**. My Father, who has given them to Me, is greater than all; and **no one is able to snatch them out of the Father's hand**. (John 10:27-29)

In these verses Jesus promises that we are **doubly held.** No can snatch us out of **His hand** or out of **Our Father's hand.** That is a comfort for us that will stay with us to the end of our lives and into eternity.

My New Life in Christ

Chapter 2 - Know We Are His
Thought Questions

1. Can we know for sure that we have eternal life? How?

2. List some verses from Scripture which confirm your answer.

My New Life in Christ
Chapter 3 - Now that We Belong to Him

Now that we belong to Him, there are some issues that **inevitably will rise** in our new life in Christ. Some of the them are: a) "**How long will this joy last**?"; b) "**What do we do when faced with temptation**?"; c) "**How do we develop Christlike character**?"; and d) "**What do we do about the Bible**?" We will explore these four questions in this chapter.

How long will this joy last?

Your joy is not an end in itself, but a result. It comes from the fact that you are in a right relationship with God through the Lord Jesus Christ.

Even **this relationship** is not an end in itself. It stems from the eternal purposes of Almighty God.

> Known to God from eternity are all His works. (Acts 15:18 NKJV)

Paul writes of Christians as those who **love God** and **are called according to His purpose**.

> And we know that God causes all things to work together for good to those who love God, to those who are called according to His purpose. (Romans 8:28)

And also, Christians **were chosen in Christ** before the foundation of the world.

> Just as He chose us in Him before the foundation of the world, that we would be holy and blameless before Him in love. (Ephesians 1:4)

We believe that our Christian lives **started** when we knelt at Calvary and it did. But at the same time, we stepped into the **everlasting pathway of the purpose of God** set in motion in eternity past.

It is important that we see this truth clearly. Humanly, we tend to think of ourselves as being **very important**. When we see ourselves in a group picture: whose face do we look for first? Of course, we look for our own.

God's view is **entirely different**. When we stand at the cross and look at life with Him, we are **not nearly** so important as we thought. Rather, **His will**, **His plan**, and **His purpose** become the main issues of our lives.

We say, "OK, I know that my joy comes from God. What if I should lose it? Then what?" Before we worry about this**, let's turn to the Word**.

> According to the eternal purpose which He accomplished in Christ Jesus our Lord... (Ephesians 3:11)

What kind of purpose is it of which we a part? An eternal purpose!

How long does an eternal purpose last? Forever and ever!

Is that long enough to see us through this life and get us to heaven? If it is, then what are we worrying about?

This is the sense of that blessed promise in Philippians...

> For I am confident of this very thing, that He who began a good work in you will perfect it until the day of Christ Jesus. (Philippians 1:6)

The term translated here "perfect" means to **bring something to a state of completion**.

God **planned** this work in us. He **initiated** it. He **will continue to do this work** until it comes to a completed state. It is tied to His almightiness and His heavenly reputation guarantees it. In light of this, we ought to trust Him with the working out of His eternal purpose.

In fact as we grow as Christians we learn by experience that God can take the most troubling circumstance and **works it out for our good**.

> For momentary, light affliction is producing for us an eternal weight of glory far beyond all comparison... (II Corinthians 4:17)

Even affliction can work for us. Paul writes in Romans 5:3-5

> And not only this, but we also exult in our tribulations, knowing that tribulation brings about perseverance; and perseverance, proven character; and proven character, hope; and hope does not disappoint, because the love of God has been poured out within our hearts through the Holy Spirit who was given to us. (Romans 5:3-5)

Since we belong to Jesus Christ, and since our lives now operate under His sovereignty; **nothing can touch our lives** without working for us, producing His good in our lives.

So we see our joy is **eternal**!

What do we do when faced with temptation?

The first thing to do about temptation is to **expect** it. There is nothing **unusual** or **abnormal** about being tempted. The person who claims that he or she is never tempted is either untruthful or deluded.

Let us get the proper approach to this matter. Not, "Why must I be tempted... go through all this testing?" Rather, "people are tempted; that much we know. We are not any different from other human beings, therefore we shall be tempted. **What provision** does God make for us?"

The Bible takes temptation for **granted**. We read about our Lord Jesus...

> For we do not have a high priest who cannot sympathize with our weaknesses, but One who **has been tempted in all things as we are**, yet without sin. (Hebrews 4:15)

He felt the **mental anguish** of that temptations carried by circumstances that arise. We read...

> For since **He Himself was tempted in that which He has suffered**, He is able to come to the aid of those who are tempted. (Hebrews 2:18)

James says that, rather than being thrown into a panic by it, we are to...

> **Consider it all joy**, my brethren, when you encounter various trials! (James 1:2)

Peter assures us that...

> Then the Lord knows how to rescue the godly from temptation, and to keep the unrighteous under punishment for the day of judgment, (II Peter 2:9)

Paul remarks that our temptation is **no different** from the testing to which everyone else is subjected...

> No temptation has overtaken you but such as is common to man; and God is faithful, who will not allow you to be tempted beyond what you are able, but with the temptation will provide the way of escape also, so that you will be able to endure it. (I Corinthians 10:13)

The Lord Jesus **teaches** us as His disciples to pray...

> And do not lead us into temptation, but deliver us from evil. For Yours is the kingdom and the power and the glory forever. Amen.' (Matthew 6:13)

The devil's business is **temptation**. He tempted the Lord Jesus – in fact, he is called the tempter in Matthew 4, and Paul calls Satan the tempter in writing to the Thessalonians.

For this reason, when I could endure it no longer, I also sent to find out about your faith, for fear that the tempter might have tempted you, and our labor would be in vain. (I Thessalonians 3:5)

Do you think the devil is going out of business just because we were converted? There is **no way**!

Learn to recognize the temptation when it comes. James says that temptation is **based upon desire**...

But each one is tempted when he is carried away and enticed by his own lust. (James 1:14)

Every one of us has certain natural desires – God made us that way. We desire food, fellowship, self-preservation, a sense of accomplishment and many other things. Then, because we are members of a sinful race, we have certain wrong desires – to cheat, and lie, and seek revenge, and try to get the better of others. These good and evil desires are mixed together in the chemistry of our souls. Satan operates on the basis of using what we already want as a means of leading us into sin.

Of course it is simple enough to recognize temptation based upon wrong desires. If it is a wrong desire, it will lead to a wrong act, and we know it. **Never** act upon a wrong desire – we will only get into more sin and trouble.

Not so easily identified, however, are temptations based on **good and legitimate desires**. Remember at the very outset that Satan is interested in taking that which is good in our lives and prostituting it to his own devilish ends. Here are a couple of questions that will help us settle the matter.

When we are about to take a course of action let us ask the following question: "**Does this glorify God**?"

> Whether, then, you eat or drink or whatever you do, do all to the glory of God. (I Corinthians 10:31)

Another question: "Can we do this **in the name of the Lord Jesus** and offer a prayer of thanksgiving over it?"

> Whatever you do in word or deed, do all in the name of the Lord Jesus, giving thanks through Him to God the Father. (Colossians 3:17)

A third question: "**Does this make me more preoccupied with "things," or does it help me to spend more time at the feet of Jesus**?"

> But the worries of the world, and the deceitfulness of riches, and the desires for other things enter in and choke the word, and it becomes unfruitful. (Mark 4:19)

A fourth question: "**Will it offend another**?"

> For through your knowledge he who is weak is ruined, the brother for whose sake Christ died. And so, by sinning against the brethren and wounding their conscience when it is weak, you sin against Christ. Therefore, if food causes my brother to stumble, I will never eat meat again, so that I will not cause my brother to stumble. (I Corinthians 8:11-13)

If we will honestly ask these questions regarding doubtful course of action, we will recognize temptation when it comes and will be prepared to **resist it** in the power that Christ gives.

Having **recognized temptation**, the next thing is to **resist it**! Let us be honest about this business. The Christian faith is not an automatic cure-all for us. If we want to go on and sin we will go on and sin and nothing will stop us. Unless we want to be different, we never will be different. And until we desire victory over temptation enough to take a stand against it, we will get nowhere.

Search our hearts today, remembering that it is "deceitful above all things, and desperately wicked" and find out the truth.

> The heart is deceitful above all things, and desperately wicked; who can know it? (Jeremiah 17:9)

An important issue we must face is: **do we want victory over temptation and sin**, or do we want an easy way to forgiveness and heaven while remaining in our sin?

Basically taking our stand **toward temptation** is like our taking our stand **with Christ**. This is nothing new, because we did it when we came for salvation. We said, "When Christ died, we died with Him, because He was dying for us. When He rose, we rose with Him, therefore, we trust Him as our Savior and identify ourselves afresh with Him for salvation." Paul writes,

> Therefore we have been buried with Him through baptism into death, so that as Christ was raised from the dead through the glory of the Father, so we too might walk in newness of life. For if we

have become united with Him in the likeness of His death, certainly we shall also be in the likeness of His resurrection, (Romans 6:4-5)

How do we develop Christlike character?

It starts with **a Person**!

The Christian life has always been a **mystery** to the unsaved. Paul writes about the unsaved man or woman's ability to understand spiritual things this way...

> But a natural man does not accept the things of the Spirit of God, for they are foolishness to him; and he cannot understand them, because they are spiritually appraised. (I Corinthians 2:14)

The natural man, **cut off** from the Spirit of God, cannot accept or receive the things of the Spirit. It is only those made alive by the Spirit can understand spiritual truth.

> That is, the mystery which has been hidden from the past ages and generations, but has now been manifested to His saints, to whom God willed to make known what is the riches of the glory of this mystery among the Gentiles, which is Christ in you, the hope of glory. (Colossians 1:26-27)

This whole truth becomes embarrassingly **simple**, once we see through it. A Person saved us, didn't He? And it takes a Person to keep us day by day. The truth is, we need Him every hour of every day.

Well if that's true, in the matter of producing **Christian character**, what makes us think we can do it on our

33

own? The all-powerful Son of God now dwells in us, and it is He who now controls the development of our lives.

The secret of Christian character is **Jesus Christ**! Living within and living out through us, His life becomes apparent where once only our failures were seen. This is what Paul means when he proclaims...

> I have been crucified with Christ; and it is no longer I who live, but Christ lives in me; and the life which I now live in the flesh I live by faith in the Son of God, who loved me and gave Himself up for me. (Galatians 2:20)

Christian character develops as we surrender to a Person!

The Lord Jesus Christ dwells in our hearts by His Holy Spirit, but **He will control only that portion** of our lives which we yield to Him. This is the reason behind Paul's words:

> Therefore I urge you, brethren, by the mercies of God, to present your bodies a living and holy sacrifice, acceptable to God, which is your spiritual service of worship. (Romans 12:1)

What do we present? **Our bodies**! Why? Because His Holy Spirit now dwells in our bodies, and the only way He can express His life and love is through **a yielded instrument**. Don't expect the Holy Spirit to transform our hearts if we refuse to let Him into all the rooms of it! Because we are Christians, we have **a right to all of the Holy Spirit** as our birthright; but the big question is: **Does He have all of us?**

This doesn't have to be a painful experience or something which we must necessarily seek. Right now, we can bow our heads and give over to God the Holy Spirit complete control of ourselves – body, soul and spirit. That is the **first step** in developing Christian character. Only He can develop it, so start by letting Him take control.

One big surprise we will experience about this time is that things for which we sought so eagerly along the line of Christian character – things like a loving heart, a generous spirit, a faithfulness in our duties, control of an unhealthy habit – are not an end in themselves, **but a result!**

The passage that presents this truth is Galatians 5:22-23.

> But the fruit of the Spirit is love, joy, peace, patience, kindness, goodness, faithfulness, gentleness, self-control; against such things there is no law. (Galatians 5:22-23)

Consider the three verses which precede this passage.

> Now the deeds of the flesh are evident, which are: immorality, impurity, sensuality, idolatry, sorcery, enmities, strife, jealousy, outbursts of anger, disputes, dissensions, factions, envying, drunkenness, carousing, and things like these, of which I forewarn you, just as I have forewarned you, that those who practice such things will not inherit the kingdom of God. (Galatians 5:19-21)

The "works of the flesh" is the **ugly title** of a very ugly list. We ought to constantly remind ourselves that all the flesh, our old Adam nature, is capable of is dead works;

actually a perversion of the good which we seek – every item on that heartbreaking list is a twisted, perverted opposite of some virtue.

"But, he says, "the fruit of the Spirit is love, joy, peace..."

Fruit, did you say, Paul?

Yes, fruit.

But **why change the figure of speech Paul**? You were speaking of the works of the flesh in those three preceding verses. **Shouldn't you now speak of the works of Spirit**?

No, he says, **not works**, for the Christian life is not mechanical, but **vital**. The life of the Holy Spirit unites with your life and produces an organic living growth. Fruit is a product of life. Christian character is never primarily the things you do – it's the person you are as a result of being indwelt by the Person – the Holy Spirit.

We obey a Person. Mary says to the servants at the wedding...

> His mother said to the servants, "Whatever He says to you, do it." (John 2:5)

She knew the secret of success when dealing **with our blessed Lord**. So did Paul. In Philippians, Paul writes...

> The things you have learned and received and heard and seen in me, practice these things, and the God of peace will be with you. (Philippians 4:9)

This verse gives us the process of finding out what God wants us to do. "**Learned**" – gained from studying God's Word. "**Received**" – gained by experience with God; "**Heard**" – gained from exhortation from the servant of God; "Seen in me" – gained from observation of true character in others.

What now? Look carefully at the next word, "**practice these things**". God will **never** force you to obey. There comes a time when, after His Spirit has dealt with you and His Word has informed you, that you must act, either to obey or to disobey. Obey Him, and you'll experience the blessed fulfillment of the promise given only to those who obey, "The God of peace will be with you."

We receive the **peace of God** when we pray about everything and commit it to Him. But we know the precious awareness of the presence of God only when we obey Him. A number of Scriptures prove this point. Peter, bold in his new experience of the Holy Spirit's power, said...

> And we are witnesses of these things; and so is the Holy Spirit, whom God has given to those who obey Him." (Acts 5:32)

Peter received the Holy Spirit in answer to the promise of the Father, according to the Word of the Lord Jesus, but he was aware of the Holy Spirit, because he was just then obeying God.

Again in Matthew, we hear the Lord Jesus saying...

> Go therefore and make disciples of all the nations, baptizing them in the name of the Father and the

Son and the Holy Spirit, teaching them to observe all that I commanded you; and lo, I am with you always, even to the end of the age." (Matthew 28:19-20)

When God is with you – because you are surrendered to Him, communing with Him, obeying – you'll be **different**, and people will know it.

Thus Samuel grew and the Lord was with him and let none of his words fail. All Israel from Dan even to Beersheba knew that Samuel was confirmed as a prophet of the Lord. (I Samuel 3:19-20)

Here are five practical **words of wisdom** on developing solid Christian character.

1. Major on Spirituality! Look for things, people, associations that help you keep your eyes **fixed on Jesus**, the Author and Finisher of our faith. Make the rule of your life Philippians 3:10...

That I may know Him and the power of His resurrection and the fellowship of His sufferings, being conformed to His death (Philippians 3:10)

That is to **KNOW HIM**, to **SHARE HIS HEART**, to **RESEMBLE HIM**, with the **MARK OF THE CROSS**.

Do not be deceived: "Evil company corrupts good habits." (I Corinthians 15:33 NKJV)

2. Expect People to Fail! When they do, as they sometimes will, they won't disappoint you. We are not talking about being cynical about everyone, but **maintain**

an awareness that "we have all sinned and fallen short of the glory of God." (Rom.3:23)

3. Always choose the high road - when faced with a choice between two courses of conduct. If there is a **better**, **more generous**, **more honest way** to do anything – take that way!

4. Strive to be more like Christ – do not strive to be like a brother or sister in Christ, but instead strive to **love Him**; **serve Him** more faithfully and become **like Him**!

5. The true Christian is the one who lives His life for Christ all the time. We cannot change our character based on our setting. We **need** to stand up for the Lord regardless of where we are and who we are with.

Character counts!

What do we do about the Bible?

We already have within us **the secret of interest** in the Bible. Whether we know it or not, we will always be **hungry for the Word of God**... because we are Christians! The person who is right with God **instinctively** loves His Word.

> O how I love Your law! It is my meditation all the day. (Psalm 119:97)
>
> How sweet are Your words to my taste! Yes, sweeter than honey to my mouth! (Psalm 119:103)

If "**Christ in you, the hope of glory**," is the secret of Christian assurance and character, it is also the basic provision for our success in the Word. The living Word dwells in your heart by faith, and His Spirit reminds us moment by moment of our need for the written Word.

The Lord Jesus was speaking expressly of **our need** for the Bible's life-giving truth when He said that the Holy Spirit would bring to us remembrance of the Scriptures.

> But the Helper, the Holy Spirit, whom the Father will send in My name, He will teach you all things, and bring to your remembrance all that I said to you. (John 14:26)

Things to remember:

1. We grow by the Word of God.

> Like newborn babies, long for the pure milk of the word, so that by it you may grow in respect to salvation, if you have tasted the kindness of the Lord. (I Peter 2:2-3)

2. We are changed by the Word.

> But we all, with unveiled face, beholding as in a mirror the glory of the Lord, are being transformed into the same image from glory to glory, just as from the Lord, the Spirit. (II Corinthians 3:18)

3. We are cleansed by the Word.

> How can a young man keep his way pure? By keeping it according to Your word. (Psalm 119:9)

4. We are kept by the Word.

Your word I have treasured in my heart, that I may not sin against You. (Psalm 119:11)

5. We share God's life through the Word.

It is the Spirit who gives life; the flesh profits nothing; the words that I have spoken to you are spirit and are life. (John 6:63)

6. We defeat the devil through the Word.

And they overcame him because of the blood of the Lamb and because of the word of their testimony, and they did not love their life even when faced with death. (Revelation 12:11)

7. We base our faith on the Word.

So faith comes from hearing, and hearing by the word of Christ. (Romans 10:17)

8. Every needed blessing is in the Word.

Seeing that His divine power has granted to us everything pertaining to life and godliness, through the true knowledge of Him who called us by His own glory and excellence! For by these He has granted to us His precious and magnificent promises, so that by them you may become partakers of the divine nature, having escaped the corruption that is in the world by lust. (II Peter 1:3-4)

Get a good **study Bible**. This Bible may include study aids like a Bible dictionary, maps of Bible lands, and a concordance. A strong commentary from a literal, historical, grammatical interpretational point of view which supports biblical inerrancy could be helpful. But the important study tool is the Bible. There are many solid translations of the Scriptures which include the New American Standard Bible, the English Standard Version and the, tried and true, New King James Version.

Make up your mind that you are going to **read your Bible regularly** until you go to glory. Make a Bible study plan and follow it. Some like finding a book of the Bible and working their way through it. A good book to start with is the Gospel of John because it tells the story of Jesus from the "beloved disciple's" perspective.

Take your time. Enjoy the investment of hours in your study. Pray for guidance from the Holy Spirit and follow His lead. The more you study, the more you will see greater amounts of detail in your study. That makes for a richer study. But again, take your time and enjoy taking in the Word regularly.

You may want to **ask your pastor for help** and suggestions for your study.

My New Life in Christ
Chapter 3 - Now that We Belong to Him
Thought Questions

1. What is one of the reasons Christians lose the joy of their salvation?

2. How can we keep the old nature from asserting itself?

3. Why do you think it is more important to try to be like Jesus than other brothers and sisters in Christ?

4. Give two reasons why the regular study is vital for our growth.

My New Life in Christ
Chapter 4 - Prayer, Fellowship, and Sharing

Three elements of your new life in Christ are **prayer**, **fellowship** and **sharing**.

Prayer

Prayer is **a cry**. Obstetricians expect newborn babes to cry out as the first evidence of life. If the child does not cry, often they will **shake** or **gently spank the newborn** to produce a cry.

Here is a singular thing. Peter says that we are "newborn babes", and yet we never expect new believers to do the very thing that a baby ought to do: **cry.**

> "Because you are sons," says Paul, "God has sent forth the Spirit of His Son into your hearts, crying out 'Abba, Father!'" (Galatians 4:6).

"Abba" is the Middle Eastern term for "**papa**". It is the cry of a childlike heart that does not know much, but knows it is alive and that it needs the tender care of a loving parent like an Abba Father.

Again, Paul says,

> For you have not received a spirit of slavery leading to fear again, but you have received a spirit of adoption as sons by which we cry out, "Abba! Father!" (Romans 8:15)

God respects the cry of the new believer's heart. There are literally hundreds of references proving this fact. Here are two:

> For he will deliver the needy when he cries for help, the afflicted also, and him who has no helper. (Psalm 72:12)

> This poor man cried, and the Lord heard him and saved him out of all his troubles. (Psalm 34:6)

Our birthright as Christians is a **warm, tender heart toward God**... that cry down deep in your spirit that reaches its poor mute hands out to God and pleads more eloquently than human words. Cherish that cry. Let it come out. Let it make itself heard in every one of your prayers, either private or public. Let us not fall into the habit of cold, formal and heartless praying.

Do you know what that cry is? It is the blessed Holy Spirit in your heart, calling out to God. Because we are Christians, He indwells us. Sometimes we do not know what to say, and yet He says it for you and God Almighty understands. Look at these beautiful words:

> In the same way the Spirit also helps our weakness; for we do not know how to pray as we should, but the Spirit Himself intercedes for us with groanings too deep for words; and He who searches the hearts knows what the mind of the Spirit is, because He intercedes for the saints according to the will of God. (Romans 8:26-27)

Let us look honestly at this matter. You are a new Christian. Sure, you do not know what to say, or how to say it. But **deep within** you dwells One who does know and whose business it is to express the very yearnings of the heart of God through your heart. That's the cry... the cry of the Holy Spirit. Prayer is a cry – His cry – to God through you!

Humanly speaking, prayer is often simply **a call for help**. Listen to Jeremiah's words...

> Call to Me and I will answer you, and I will tell you great and mighty things, which you do not know. (Jeremiah 33:3)

This is encouraging. A call means an earnest desire, a determined desperate desire – and thank God, a call to Him means an answer.

> For whoever will call on the name of the Lord will be saved. (Romans 10:13)

Form a habit of calling on God at every occasion of need in your life. A bowed head, an open heart, and the simple words, "Lord Jesus, help me now!" can mean the difference between defeat and victory.

Prayer involves **confession** and **cleansing**.

> If I regard wickedness in my heart, the Lord will not hear; (Psalm 66:18)

Isaiah sounds the same warning:

> Behold, the Lord's hand is not so short that it cannot save; nor is His ear so dull that it cannot hear. But your iniquities have made a separation

between you and your God, and your sins have hidden His face from you so that He does not hear. (Isaiah 59:1-2)

Make up your mind to this now: I can **never hide** known sin in my heart and expect to get my prayers answered.

Do you know how to get rid of sin? **Confess it** and **forsake it**.

He who conceals his transgressions will not prosper, but he who confesses and forsakes them will find compassion. (Proverbs 28:13)

If we confess our sins, He is faithful and righteous to forgive us our sins and to cleanse us from all unrighteousness. (I John 1:9)

Just **tell God the truth** about your sin. Specific confession will bring specific cleansing. And, of course, when you have sinned against an individual, you will go get right with that person, too.

Like everything else in the Christian life, prayer must be **Christ-centered**. The disciples, beginners in the school of prayer, were told:

Until now you have asked for nothing in My name; ask and you will receive, so that your joy may be made full. (John 16:24)

Why is this? Look at the preceding verse...

In that day you will not question Me about anything. Truly, truly, I say to you, if you ask the

Father for anything in My name, He will give it to you. (John 16:23)

"In Jesus' name", we say when we pray – **Why?**

Because that is the saving Name:

> She will bear a Son; and you shall call His name Jesus, for He will save His people from their sins." (Matthew 1:21)

This is because He is the **only One though Whom** we can come to God.

> Jesus said to him, "I am the way, and the truth, and the life; no one comes to the Father but through Me." (John 14:6)

It is because He is the One whose work today is **interceding for us**, pleading for us before the Father.

> Therefore He is able also to save forever those who draw near to God through Him, since He always lives to make intercession for them. (Hebrews 7:25)

The Bible tells us to **come boldly** to the **throne of grace** when we need help.

> Let us therefore come boldly to the throne of grace, that we may obtain mercy and find grace to help in time of need. (Heb.4:16 NKJV)

Fellowship

Fellowship is another *important subject* for you in your new life in Christ. We not only experience a new birth, but we are born into a new family as we receive the Lord Jesus as our Savior. As a result, we have a new relationship with God the Father, with Jesus as Lord, with the Holy Spirit in His indwelling presence and are spiritually related to every believer in Christ as brothers and sisters in faith.

The Apostle John writes...

> What we have seen and heard we proclaim to you also, so that you too may have fellowship with us; and indeed our fellowship is with the Father, and with His Son Jesus Christ. These things we write, so that our joy may be made complete. (I John 1:3-4)

This passage teaches that God intended for us to **enjoy the fellowship of other believers**. This fellowship is always to be centered on our personal relationship with Christ. The word for fellowship in the Greek language is **KOINONIA** and it describes a very special new relationship of sharing identity, function and purpose with one another.

As we think of the vital relationship that started immediately at the beginning of the church in the book of Acts. We see that one of the keys of the tremendous witness for Christ was KOINONIA or **fellowship**.

> They were continually devoting themselves to the apostles' teaching and to fellowship, to the

breaking of bread and to prayer. Everyone kept feeling a sense of awe; and many wonders and signs were taking place through the apostles. And all those who had believed were together and had all things in common; (Acts 2:42-44)

Day by day continuing with one mind in the temple, and breaking bread from house to house, they were taking their meals together with gladness and sincerity of heart, praising God and having favor with all the people. And the Lord was adding to their number day by day those who were being saved. (Acts 2:46-47)

This type of fellowship is **hard** for us to understand. We live in a depersonalized world where we have to remember user numbers, passwords, student ID numbers, employee ID numbers, shopping ID numbers and PINs to establish identity and gain access to properties and accounts. In a highly-computerized society there is a **great need** for authentic fellowship. Something beyond being just Facebook friends!

Fellowship means **sharing a life** with someone. It means there is one life flowing through all those who have found new life in Christ. The early church was well-aware of their oneness in Christ. They had one life which pulsed through each of their hearts.

The basis for our fellowship – for this KOINONIA is the **living, risen, resurrected Christ**. Jesus is alive and our fellowship with Him is real now and will be forever. Christ's fellowship is the greatest fellowship that has ever existed on the face of the earth

The oneness that Jesus puts in our hearts, the oneness with other believers is something special to know and to experience. We find that wherever we go in the world, if we run into a person who has received the living, resurrected Christ, **we have a bond**. We are brothers and sisters with each other even if we speak different languages and come from different cultures.

Within minutes, we **develop a rapport** with these family members that is not found among other people. Why? It is because we share the same light from Heaven. We have the same hope because we worship the same Christ.

Our fellowship (KOINONIA) is "with Him" John tells us...

> If we say that we have fellowship with Him and yet walk in the darkness, we lie and do not practice the truth; (I John 1:6)

The fellowship we have with Him is leading to **a life lived in the Light**. It is so much the fact that we can see if we walk in darkness, perhaps it suggests that we do not really have genuine fellowship.

This is one way we are assured we have come to know Him. It is evidenced by what we share in our relationship with God which includes His sharing of eternal life in us.

> I have been crucified with Christ; and it is no longer I who live, but Christ lives in me; and the life which I now live in the flesh I live by faith in the Son of God, who loved me and gave Himself up for me. (Galatians 2:20)

We have this **mutual participation**, and what a blessed fellowship it is – having descended **vertically** from God and now is established **horizontally** with brothers and sisters in Christ here on Earth.

There are two ordinances that the Church has been commanded to observe: **communion** and **water baptism**. Both of these ordinances show in picture form the precious fellowship we share with each other.

Communion, which comes from the same root word as KOINONIA, celebrates on a regular basis the **perfect person** and **work of Jesus Christ**. The bread is distributed through the Church and depicts the holiness of our Savior. He was the Holy Lamb of God who takes away our sin. John writes about John the Baptist expression when he first recognized Jesus, the Messiah...

> The next day he saw Jesus coming to him and said, "Behold, the Lamb of God who takes away the sin of the world!" (John 1:29)

He was the spotless sacrifice without sin and therefore was the only acceptable sacrifice to satisfy the justice of God. The cup of the juice of the grape **portrays** the work of Christ. Jesus became the atoning substitute for sin as the judgment for the whole world's sin was poured out on Jesus at Calvary.

> He made Him who knew no sin to be sin on our behalf, so that we might become the righteousness of God in Him. (II Corinthians 5:21)

When we have this fellowship it creates **a real joy** in our hearts. Our joy becomes **fuller** and **richer** when we experience fellowship with one another. It is God's purpose in every believer's life that we seek and maintain fellowship with other believers.

As new believers **we must connect** with other believers in a local church. We need that fellowship of worshippers of God who have also experienced the new birth. Sadly not every church fits that requirement. We can only have authentic KOINONIA with people who really **know** the Lord. So we must seek the Lord's guidance to find a place in a local body of believers who share a living relationship with Jesus Christ.

Water Baptism pictures the believer identifying with the **death**, **burial** and **resurrection** of the Lord Jesus Christ. Water Baptism is a symbolic witness of the inward work that was done in a believer's life when they received Jesus Christ as Savior. We are urged to demonstrate our faith publicly by being baptized. When we find a Bible-preaching, Bible-believing Church, we should inquire about baptism so we can testify to the change that has taken place since Jesus saved us.

So these two ordinances are to be honored and followed by the Church corporately and us individually.

The Bible says we should **enjoy** and **not forsake the gathering** of Christians so that we may encourage one another...

> And let us consider how to stimulate one another to love and good deeds, not forsaking our own assembling together, as is the habit of some, but encouraging one another; and all the more as you see the day drawing near. (Hebrews 10:24-25)

Stay in the Light! As a new believer, I encourage you to seek the Lord in finding a Christian fellowship and get serious about developing your relationship with the Lord and others in His body. Get honest with Him and with one another. What blessings you will find!

If you have not yet found a church where Jesus Christ is lifted up and honored, where His Word is believed and proclaimed, then I encourage you to **find such a church** and **enter fully** into the services. Take advantage of the opportunities of worship and study available to you there. God will richly bless you through His Word and the fellowship of other believers in Christ if you do.

Sharing

Share this new life that Christ has given you.
Do I have to testify of my new faith in Christ? My reaction to that question is "How can you help it?" True testimony consists of vastly more than the spoken word. If you are real and honest about your new faith in Jesus Christ it is going to come out.

It is important to keep in mind: whether you are in the will of God or not, whether saved or unsaved, you are most emphatically giving a witness to **whatever rules your life**. Like it or not, some of us are witnessing to our own selfishness, our laziness, our lusts, our shallowness, our pride and a thousand other things!

You never successfully **conceal** anything. You are witness to whatever you are down deep in your heart.

> You brood of vipers, how can you, being evil, speak what is good? For the mouth speaks out of that which fills the heart. (Matthew 12:34)

I had friend who used to say, "**What's down in the well, comes up in the bucket!**"

There is a **tendency** to leave all witnessing to a pastor or a church leader that is not based a lack of God's enablement as much as it is a sign of sheer laziness or lack of courage to share the truth.

Notice the **significance** of Acts 1:8 in this connection. The disciples had so far been witnesses only to their own cowardice and fear; to their low viewpoint of the Kingdom as a restore-Israel type of program; and to their totally narrow point of view' so far as help for the world was concerned. Before Jesus ascends into Heaven to sit down at the Father's right hand He said to the Church to be...

> But you will receive power when the Holy Spirit has come upon you; and you shall be My witnesses both in Jerusalem, and in all Judea and Samaria, and even to the remotest part of the earth." (Acts 1:8)

Successful witnessing never was a matter of determination on the part of the early church. They never did urge each other to testify. It was not a matter of conscience even. They simply **reacted normally to the lordship** of the Holy Spirit. They were genuine. Even in their failure before and immediately after Calvary, they were utterly and plainly honest. When the Spirit came upon them and began to speak through them, it was not a matter of trying but of glad surrender to His presence and power.

What they were was **willing**! Willing to be led by the Spirit! They purposed, as the Spirit led, to pray every day for God's grace, to read the Word together regularly, share communion and fellowship with one another.

> They were continually devoting themselves to the apostles' teaching and to fellowship, to the breaking of bread and to prayer. (Acts 2:42)

Share Christ! Rely on His will and His Spirit when it comes to the matter of a relationship so important that it involves the salvation of a precious soul. Why, do you think, did the Lord Jesus emphasize so often the fact that the Holy Spirit would be given to guide, to bring to remembrance His words, to put proper words into the disciples' mouths, to teach them what to say? Was it not that the Lord Jesus knows weakness of the human brain, the waywardness of the human tongue and the impossibility of changing lives by mere talk?

A staged witness is **an act of perjury**! The best witness is spontaneous and honest. What you are will lead to what you say. Get in touch with the Lord Jesus Christ. Pray with Him often as He leads. Take in the Word of God on a regular basis personally and in a church setting.

When we live consistently in this deep fellowship with our Lord and others, **our life testifies**. He wants you, in a broken-hearted, sincere, now-and-forever kind of surrender that will make an effective Christian witness out of everything you say and do.

In sharing Christ with others who do not know Him yet, there are a **few thoughts** to keep in mind.

1. Don't talk religion to people. Actually we talk to people all day long about almost every conceivable topic. We need to resolve to be willing to speak naturally about the greatest subject in the world, the Lord Jesus Christ, whenever we have the opportunity to choose the topic of conversation.

2. Fill our minds and hearts with the Word of God.

> I will also speak of Your testimonies before kings and shall not be ashamed. (Psalm 119:46)

We speak naturally about subjects that have gotten down into our below-routine level of thinking. Hide God's Word in our hearts and we will find ourselves speaking of it, living by it, illustrating truth by our character and conduct and this will help in becoming effective witnesses for Christ.

Memorize key verses that can be of assistance in explaining the Gospel. Choose a few from our list of Scripture references in the appendix and commit them to memory. How can you do that? Select a verse that you want to recall word-for-word, read it over and over on the first day, and then review it once a day for seven weeks. At the end of that time you will have the Scripture, but – more important – it will have you!

3. Begin each day with prayer for God's guidance, and form a habit of watching throughout the day for the people God will send to us for our ministry

to them. He knows who we can help, and He can put us in touch with them.

4. Always rely on the Holy Spirit to tell us what to say. Pray before we begin the conversations. The Holy Spirit will lead us to use a Scripture, a telling thought that just may add a link in a chain of events that may lead someone to receiving Christ. The Holy Spirit does the work of regeneration; our job is being a witness of what He does to someone who needs to trust in Jesus.

5. Always press gently for some action now. It may be only a word of prayer where we are talking together... or it may be we will have the joy of leading our friend directly to a saving knowledge of Jesus Christ. Depend on the Lord's lead to see if God is moving this person closer to coming to know the Lord.

6. Follow through! One contact may mean attention; another appreciation; but a third often could mean a decision.

7. Soul-winning is a miracle. To try it in the energy of the flesh is fraudulent and sinful. God must do it through us, and He will, on the basis of Colossians 2:6 and Philippians 2:13.

> Therefore as you have received Christ Jesus the Lord, so walk in Him, (Colossians 2:6)

> For it is God who is at work in you, both to will and to work for His good pleasure. (Philippians 2:13)

We received Christ by faith, now let Him **operate though us in faith**. When Jesus wins a soul, the work is well done! Listen to His words...

> "I have manifested Your name to the men whom You gave Me out of the world; they were Yours and You gave them to Me, and they have kept Your word. Now they have come to know that everything You have given Me is from You; for the words which You gave Me I have given to them; and they received them and truly understood that I came forth from You, and they believed that You sent Me. I ask on their behalf; I do not ask on behalf of the world, but of those whom You have given Me; for they are Yours; and all things that are Mine are Yours, and Yours are Mine; and I have been glorified in them. I am no longer in the world; and yet they themselves are in the world, and I come to You. Holy Father, keep them in Your name, the name which You have given Me, that they may be one even as We are. While I was with them, I was keeping them in Your name which You have given Me; and I guarded them and not one of them perished but the son of perdition, so that the Scripture would be fulfilled." (John 17:6-12)

So we realize that our new life in Christ includes the important aspects of **prayer**, **fellowship**, and **sharing**.

My New Life in Christ

Chapter 4 - Prayer, Fellowship, and Sharing
Thought Questions

1. Why do we pray in Jesus' name?

2. Define KOINONIA in your own words.

3. What is the difference between Christian fellowship and any other kind of fellowship?

4. Why do I have to testify of my new faith in Christ?

My New Life in Christ
A Final Word

The sudden change that occurs in the life of one who chooses Christ as Savior is **only the beginning** of a totally new experience. The new Christian realizes that somehow he is **different**, but often that sense of difference is swallowed up in confusion. At this crucial time sound biblical instruction is essential.

This book's writing has endeavored to provide clear teaching on basic themes selected with new believers in mind. **My New Life in Christ** has offered counsel drawn from biblical truth and genuine experience. The subjects brought under consideration included the good news about eternal life, knowing we are His, now that we belong to Him, facing temptation, lasting joy, development of Christian character, prayer, fellowship, Bible study and knowing God's will.

It is exciting to have and hold a new life in Christ. May the Lord richly bless this new life with all the deep joy, undiminished peace, and unfailing love that is the birthright of all of us who know Jesus!

My New Life in Christ

Memory verses

Salvation belongs to the Lord; Your blessing be upon Your people! Selah. (Psalm 3:8)

The Lord is my light and my salvation; whom shall I fear? The Lord is the defense of my life; whom shall I dread? (Psalm 27:1)

Surely His salvation is near to those who fear Him, That glory may dwell in our land. (Psalm 85:9)

He put on righteousness like a breastplate, and a helmet of salvation on His head; and He put on garments of vengeance for clothing and wrapped Himself with zeal as a mantle. (Isaiah 59:17)

For my eyes have seen Your salvation, (Luke 2:30)

And Jesus said to him, "Today salvation has come to this house, because he, too, is a son of Abraham. (Luke 19:9)

But as many as received Him, to them He gave the right to become children of God, even to those who believe in His name, (John 1:12)

Jesus answered and said to him, "Truly, truly, I say to you, unless one is born again he cannot see the kingdom of God." (John 3:3)

"For God so loved the world, that He gave His [a]only begotten Son, that whoever believes in Him shall not perish, but have eternal life. (John 3:16)

He who believes in Him is not judged; he who does not believe has been judged already, because he has not believed in the name of the only begotten Son of God. (John 3:18)

And there is salvation in no one else; for there is no other name under heaven that has been given among men by which we must be saved." (Acts 4:12)

For I am not ashamed of the gospel, for it is the power of God for salvation to everyone who believes, to the Jew first and also to the Greek. (Romans 1:16)

For all have sinned and fall short of the glory of God. (Romans 3:23)

Therefore, having been justified by faith, we have peace with God through our Lord Jesus Christ, (Romans 5:1)

For the wages of sin is death, but the free gift of God is eternal life in Christ Jesus our Lord. (Romans 6:23)

for with the heart a person believes, resulting in righteousness, and with the mouth he confesses, resulting in salvation. (Romans 10:10)

So faith comes from hearing, and hearing by the word of Christ. (Romans 10:17)

Therefore if anyone is in Christ, he is a new creature; the old things passed away; behold, new things have come. (II Corinthians 5:17)

He made Him who knew no sin to be sin on our behalf, so that we might become the righteousness of God in Him. (II Corinthians 5:21)

For He says, "At the acceptable time I listened to you, And on the day of salvation I helped you." Behold, now is "the acceptable time," behold, now is "the day of salvation" (II Corinthians 6:2)

I have been crucified with Christ; and it is no longer I who live, but Christ lives in me; and the life which I now live in the flesh I live by faith in the Son of God, who loved me and gave Himself up for me. (Gal.2:20)

And that from childhood you have known the sacred writings which are able to give you the wisdom that leads to salvation through faith which is in Christ Jesus. (II Timothy 3:15)

Knowing that you were not redeemed with perishable things like silver or gold from your futile way of life inherited from your forefathers, but with precious blood, as of a lamb unblemished and spotless, the blood of Christ. (I Peter 1:18-19)

These things I have written to you who believe in the name of the Son of God, so that you may know that you have eternal life. (I John 5:13)

My New Life in Christ
Answer Key – Possible Answers Given

Chapter 1 - The Good News about Eternal Life
Thought Questions

1. How do we know that we are born again?

Answer - I have experienced a new birth, a moment where I trusted that Christ's work on the cross paid for my sins. We believed that Christ died for me.

2. How can we know that we have eternal life?

Answer - By believing in Jesus Christ as my personal Lord and Savior, I can claim this because God has given me His Word that "...as many as received Him, to them He gave the right to become children of God, even to those who believe in His name." (John 1:12)

Chapter 2 - Know We Are His
Thought Questions

1. Can we know for sure that we have eternal life? How?

Answer – Yes, when we place our faith in the Lord Jesus Christ for salvation and trust Him, we are forever held by a grip that is stronger than any force in the universe. It is God's grasp on us forever!

In these verses Jesus promises that we are doubly held. No can snatch us out of His hand or out of Our Father's hand. That is a comfort for us that will stay with us to the end of our lives and into eternity.

2. List some verses from Scripture which confirm your answer.

Answer – For example - John 1:12, John 3:16, John 10:27-29

Chapter 3 - Prayer, Fellowship, and Sharing Thought Questions

1. What is one of the reasons Christians lose the joy of their salvation?

Answer – One reason Christians struggle with remembering their joy is permanent is when some tragic circumstance surfaces: the death of a loved one, a sudden loss of a job or a possession, a personal crisis experienced by the person or a loved one. The cure is to again to fix our eyes on Jesus, the Author and Finisher of our Faith. (See Hebrews 12:2) His joy remains regardless of the struggle He permits in our lives. That is a testimony of His Spirit's work and His grace.

2. How can we keep the old nature from asserting itself?

Answer – Romans 6 helps with this challenge. Take time to study this important chapter. The key idea is that we must exercise the practice of continually yielding our members, our bodies, as instruments of righteousness unto God for His service and to continue to reckon ourselves dead to sin and its influences.

3. Why do you think it is more important to try to be like Jesus than other brothers and sisters in Christ?

Answer – Jesus is the standard that never changes or comes short. Our desire as we grow is to become more like our Savior. Even strong brothers and sisters in Christ will let us down from time to time. Jesus never fails!

4. Give two reasons why regular study is vital for our growth.

Answer – Here is a good answer to this questions from the website – "Got Questions"

We should read and study the Bible because it is God's Word to us. The Bible is literally "God-breathed" (II Timothy 3:16). In other words, it is God's very words to us. There are so many questions that philosophers have asked that God answers for us in Scripture. What is the purpose to life? Where did I come from? Is there life after death? How do I get to heaven? Why is the world full of evil? Why do I struggle to do good? In addition to these "big" questions, the Bible gives much practical advice in areas such as: What do I look for in a mate? How can I have a successful marriage? How can I be a good friend? How can I be a good parent? What is success and how do I achieve it? How can I change? What really matters in life? How can I live so that I do not look back with regret? How can I handle the unfair circumstances and bad events of life victoriously? (**Got Questions** - Why should we read the Bible / study the Bible?)

Chapter 4 - Prayer, Fellowship, and Sharing
Thought Questions

1. Why do we pray in Jesus' name?

Answer – The short answer is because Jesus told us to!

> Whatever you ask in My name, that will I do, so
> that the Father may be glorified in the Son. If you
> ask Me anything in My name, I will do it. (John
> 14:13-14)

"In Jesus name" is not just a tag we add to each prayer,
we are asking our request because of Who Jesus is and
based on His authority and position. We are asking for
God's will to be done in every circumstance and the Lord
Jesus is the center of that will. We only have access to
God based on our relationship with Jesus Christ.

2. Define KOINONIA in your own words.

Answer – KOINONIA is fellowship, sharing things in
common, have a communion of fellowship with each
other. It is a relationship based on the deep connection
we have with one another. There is KOINONIA with the
Lord for the believer in Jesus Christ. (I John 1:7) and
there is KOINONIA with fellow believers because of our
shared identity in the family of God. (Acts 2:42)

3. What is the difference between Christian fellowship and
any other kind of fellowship?

Answer – The difference is the spiritual component that is
part of brothers and sisters in Christ. Grace changes

everything and it transforms our interpersonal relationships too.

4. Why do I have to testify of my new faith in Christ?

Answer – The Bible tells us to be ready to give a defense of the hope that is within us.

> But sanctify Christ as Lord in your hearts, always being ready to make a defense to everyone who asks you to give an account for the hope that is in you, yet with gentleness and reverence; (I Peter 3:15)

We need to be ready to tell others about our new faith. From the Apostle Paul's example, part of that defense should be the story of how Christ saved us. Maybe write down our testimony to help us collect the events and thoughts you had as you were being led to Christ so you can share with others what happened to you.

Made in the USA
Middletown, DE
14 October 2023